NATURE PROJECTS FOR EVERY SEASON

SPRING

by Phyllis S. Busch

illustrated by Megan Halsey

BENCHMARK BOOKS

MARSHALL CAVENDISH
NEW YORK

For my dear friend
Richard Grossman
— P. S. B.

To my father
— M. H.

Benchmark Books
Marshall Cavendish Corporation
99 White Plains Road
Tarrytown, NY 10591-9001

Printed in Hong Kong

First Edition

Library of Congress Cataloging-in-Publication Data
Busch, Phyllis S.
Spring / by Phyllis S. Busch ; illustrated by Megan Halsey.
p. cm. — (Nature projects for every season)
Includes bibliographical references (p.) and index.
Summary: Explains what spring is like, and why it occurs. Includes indoor and outdoor projects.
ISBN 0-7614-0986-6
1. Nature study—Activity programs—Juvenile literature. 2. Spring—Juvenile literature.
[1. Nature Study. 2. Spring.] I. Halsey, Megan, ill. II. Title. III. Series.
QH81.B9934   1999   98-49413   508.2—dc21   CIP   AC

CONTENTS

WHY WE HAVE SEASONS

We live on a planet called Earth. Earth is constantly spinning round and round. It makes a complete turn every day. Earth faces the Sun part of the time. Part of the time it turns away from the Sun as it spins. The side of Earth away from the Sun has night, and on the side facing the Sun, it is day.

Our planet does not spin straight up and down. It always slants to one side. We say that Earth tilts as it spins.

The tilting Earth makes a big loop around the Sun at the same time that it spins around every twenty-four hours. It takes Earth a whole year to make its long journey around the Sun.

The spring season arrives here as the traveling Earth tilts toward the Sun. Summer follows spring. Autumn comes next as Earth tips away from the Sun. The winter season follows autumn. A whole year passes by the time Earth has gone through all the four seasons. Then the tilting, spinning planet Earth begins its voyage around the Sun all over again. It is the beginning of another year.

Now you know why we have seasons. We have seasons because the spinning Earth is always tilted in the same direction as it goes around the Sun.

SPRING

Spring is on its way when the days begin to grow longer. The snow melts and the air feels warmer. The first day of spring arrives about March 21.

There are twelve hours of daytime and twelve hours of nighttime on the first day of spring. After that the days continue to grow longer and the nights become shorter. This happens because Earth is now pointing more to the Sun, and our part of it is leaning closer to the Sun.

the first day of spring

sun

earth tilts towards sun

spring

The longer sunny days warm the earth. Spring rains wet
the soil. The season suddenly becomes full of new life. Plants
begin to grow. Many different birds and butterflies appear.
Woodchucks, chipmunks, and other, larger animals emerge
from their winter homes. The air is filled with fresh smells,
new sounds, many different colors. You will surely want to
explore what you find on the ground. But there is much that
is interesting overhead and under your feet.

Spring is a great time for outdoor science and nature activities.
And there are many ways to carry on further projects indoors.

OUTDOOR ACTIVITIES

LOOKING FOR ROBIN REDBREAST

You know that spring is here when you see your first robin. Most robins have gone south for the winter. They return in the spring. Male robins are the first to come back. The males have black heads and bright yellow bills. Their breasts are the color of red bricks.

As soon as the robins arrive they begin to eat. Watch them peck at the ground. See them pull up fat earthworms. In a few days they begin to sing. Listen for their sweet songs very early in the morning and again in the evening. They also sing cheerfully before it rains.

Female robins arrive about a week later. They have paler breasts and gray heads. Soon the male and female robins pair off. Each couple builds a nest. The mother robin will lay her four blue eggs in the nest. She will sit on the eggs to keep them warm until they hatch. Look for baby robins in about two weeks.

Robins often build nests near the homes of people. Try to find a robin's nest. Then you may watch it every day to find out what goes on there.

female (mother)

baby robins hatching

nest

male (father)

worm

MAKE SOME SOIL

Examine the ground around you. You will find soil and rocks of different sizes. Soil comes mostly from crumbling rock. Try to make some soil.

Find a spot of bare soil. Dig around to find a few stones. Select two stones that look alike and rub them together over a piece of paper. Do this for fifteen minutes. The little pieces that are rubbed off are soil particles. How much soil did you make?

Use some measuring spoons to find out. You also discovered that it was slow, hard work.

Find pairs of different kinds of stones. Try to turn these into soil. You will find that some kinds crumble more easily than others.

There are many ways in which soil forms naturally. One way is when wind or water pushes rocks against each other, crushing the rocks.

stones & rocks

soil

measuring spoons

FINDING EARTHWORMS AT HOME

Earthworms spend winter in the unfrozen soil below. They crawl above the ground when warm spring weather arrives. They feed their way up by making little tunnels or burrows. They eat bits of dead plants. The earthworm leaves a hole in the soil when it pokes above the ground.

You can find where earthworms live by searching for a patch of soil with many holes. It looks as if someone made these holes with a pencil.

Look a little closer to find very small balls of soil around each opening. The little balls are waste matter. They are called castings. Castings make the soil very rich.

A good time to find earthworms is on cloudy or rainy days. The worms have to leave their tunnels to keep from drowning.

Try to make some of the worms leave their holes. Pour a little water down a few earthworm holes.

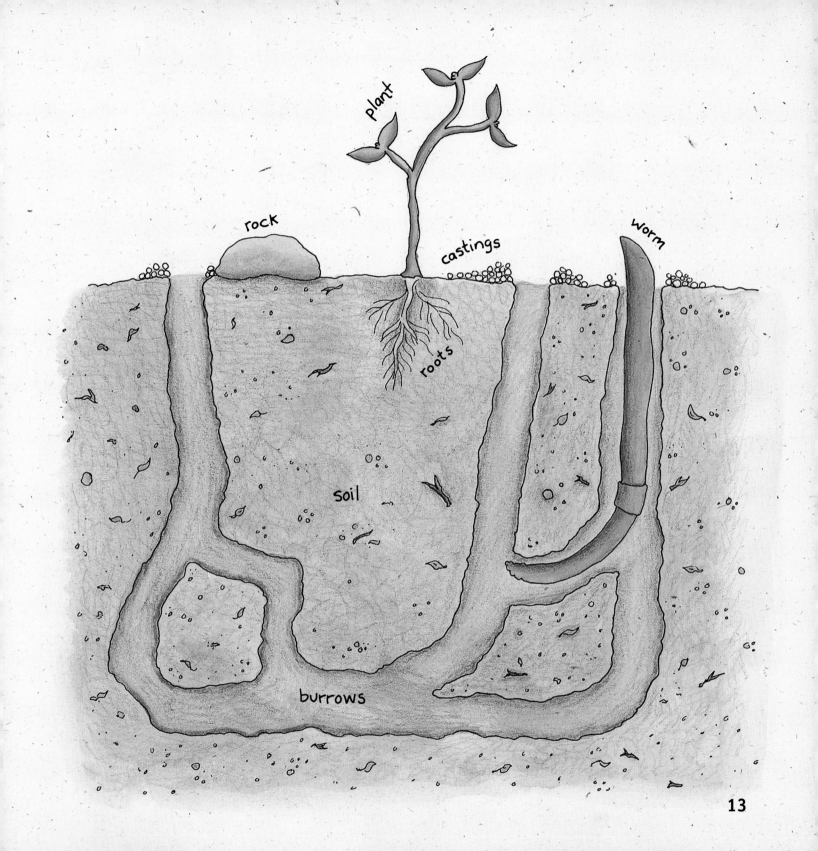

13

PAINTING WITH DANDELIONS

Look for dandelions on a sunny day in May. You will find the golden flowers everywhere. They grow in vacant lots and in gardens. You will find them in lawns and along the sides of the roads. They bloom in the fields as well as in the cracks of your driveway. The flowers look pretty and smell sweet.

You can use the yellow in the flower to paint pictures. Pick a little bouquet of dandelions. Add some of the plant's green leaves.

Draw a picture of a dandelion flower on a piece of paper. Draw some leaves on your picture. Now remove the yellow flower head from one of the dandelions. Use it as a paintbrush. Rub the flower onto your sketch of the flower. The yellow dye in the flower will paint your flower a bright golden color.

Use the green plant leaves in the same way to paint the leaves of your picture.

bouquet

leaves

dandelion heads

14

WATCHING TENT CATERPILLARS

Look up among the tree branches to find a tent caterpillar nest. The nest looks like a mass of gray webs. It is spun of a fine light silk. It is easier to spot these nests in early spring before the leaves are fully grown.

The caterpillars will turn into dark brown moths by the middle of summer. The nest is used only as long as the insect remains a caterpillar. Caterpillars leave the tent three times a day, only for meals. They feed on the leaves of the tree where they have spun their nest.

Each caterpillar spins a trail of silk as it crawls along the branches. It uses this trail to guide it back to its nest after feeding. Look for these trail guides and for feeding insects. You will find them mostly in cherry trees, but you can find them in other trees as well.

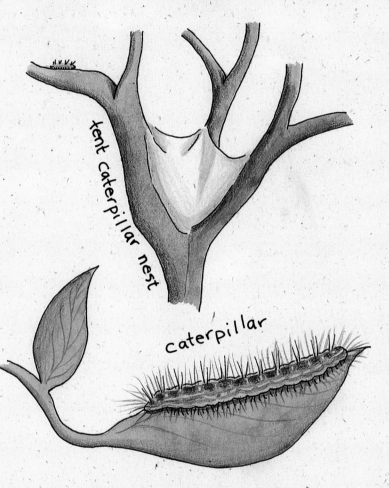

tent caterpillar nest

caterpillar

moth

HOW MANY DIFFERENT COLORS CAN YOU FIND OUTDOORS?

Close your eyes and think of all the colors you might find outdoors. There are probably more colors than you think. Here is a way to find out. Make a collection of as many colors as you can find. Cut pieces of different colors from construction paper, colored paper pads, colored yarns, pieces of fabric, pieces of wallpaper. You can also get colored samples from paint shops. Add more colors from your magic markers and crayons.

Take your collection of assorted colors outdoors. What can you find to match each of your colors? Examine everything. Look at all parts of trees, bushes, and flowers. Check the soil, pebbles, rocks, and the ground. Also look at litter, people, and animals. Check out the sky and anything in the air.

How many different colors did you find? Spring, even early spring, is a very colorful season of the year.

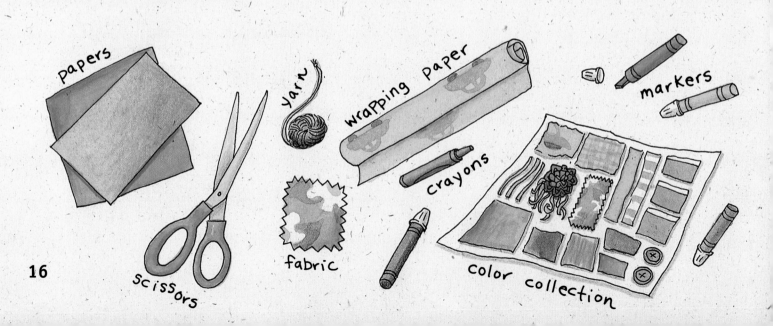

papers

yarn

wrapping paper

markers

crayons

fabric

scissors

color collection

16

flowers

butterfly

cloud

flower

twigs

salamander

pebbles

BUBBLEGUM

found items

dandelion

ONE ticket

stones

chipmunk

leaves

17

DISCOVER THE FIRST BUTTERFLIES

The mourning cloak butterflies are the first spring butterflies. Look for them in March. It may be quite chilly. There may even be snow on the ground. You can find these large brown butterflies resting on a tree in a patch of sunlight. Sometimes you may find them feeding on tree sap that is dripping from a broken branch.

The mourning cloak looks like a piece of tree bark when its wings are closed. It may be almost as wide as your hand when its wings are open.

It is very handsome when it spreads its wings. The edge of its wings has a golden border. Inside the border is a row of bright blue dots.

mourning cloak butterfly

MEASURE THE AMOUNT OF RAINFALL

Clouds are made up of tiny drops of water. These drops grow larger and larger. They get heavier as they grow. Finally the drops become too heavy to stay up as clouds. The sun disappears and the sky becomes darker. It looks as if one large gray cloud covers the whole sky. The drops of water begin to fall. It is raining.

Here is how you can find out how much rain has fallen during a rainstorm. Place a large measuring cup in an open space away from trees or buildings when it starts to rain. You can see how much water is in the cup after the rain has stopped.

You can also use the cup to measure how much rain falls in ten or fifteen minutes during the storm.

Another interesting thing to measure is whether the same amount of rain falls everywhere. Take a number of clean cans or jars and put them in different places outdoors. You can then use the measuring cup to find out how much water is in each container. Do they all have the same amount of water? If the amounts are different, can you figure out why some have more rainfall than others?

rain cloud

measuring cup

frontstep   backyard   drive

jars   19

HUNT FOR SPRING PEEPERS

You know that spring has really arrived when you hear the chorus of spring peepers. It sounds like the tinkling of little bells.

Spring peepers are tiny brownish frogs that are no larger than your thumb. Each has the mark of a dark brown cross on its back. You can hear the peepers call by day but they call much louder at night. Plan to search for spring peepers after sunset.

Carry a flashlight. It would also be wise to wear boots, since the frogs live in wet places. Find a watery place such as a large puddle or a pond. The peepers may stop singing as you approach them. Be very quiet and patient. They will soon continue their sweet chorus,

peep peep peep. Watch their throats blow up like little balloons when they sing. The males are singing to attract the females.

The female frogs lay their eggs in April. The eggs look like bits of colorless jelly. Each egg is attached singly on the leaves of plants under the water.

"peep, peep, peep"

"peep, peep, peep"

eggs

FIND THE FIRST SPRING FLOWER

The earliest flower to appear in the spring is called the skunk cabbage. You will find these wildflowers in wet places along a road or in the woods. Look for little points sticking above the ground. They are about the size and shape of ice cream cones turned upside down. They are colored purple, green, and brown. You can imagine that they resemble very small creatures from outer space.

The colorful hoods protect the tiny skunk cabbage flowers that bloom inside, under the hood. These flowers give off heat. The heat melts the snow or frozen ground above. This makes it possible for the plant to grow up. It will develop large leaves that look like the leaves of a cabbage. Tear off a small piece of leaf and smell it. You will find out why this plant was named skunk cabbage.

growing skunk cabbages

21

OBSERVE SOME VERY BUSY ANTS

Many kinds of animals live underground beneath your feet. One of the most interesting is a little insect known as the sidewalk ant. It builds its home under rocks or stones or paved driveways.

Examine the ground to find some little piles of sand or soil with a little hole in the middle of the pile. You can also find these small hills between the cracks of sidewalks in the city. Look closely and you will find ants, busy crawling in and out of the hole. Look more carefully to see each ant carrying a grain of sand out of the hole. It drops its load on the pile, then crawls right back down the hole.

This goes on all day until about four o'clock in the afternoon. The march continues, but now the ants are taking the sand back into the nest. What is going on? The sand or soil grains get damp during the night. The ants remove them by day so that the moist particles can dry out in the sun. The grains are returned in the afternoon to provide the ants with a warm, dry bed for the night.

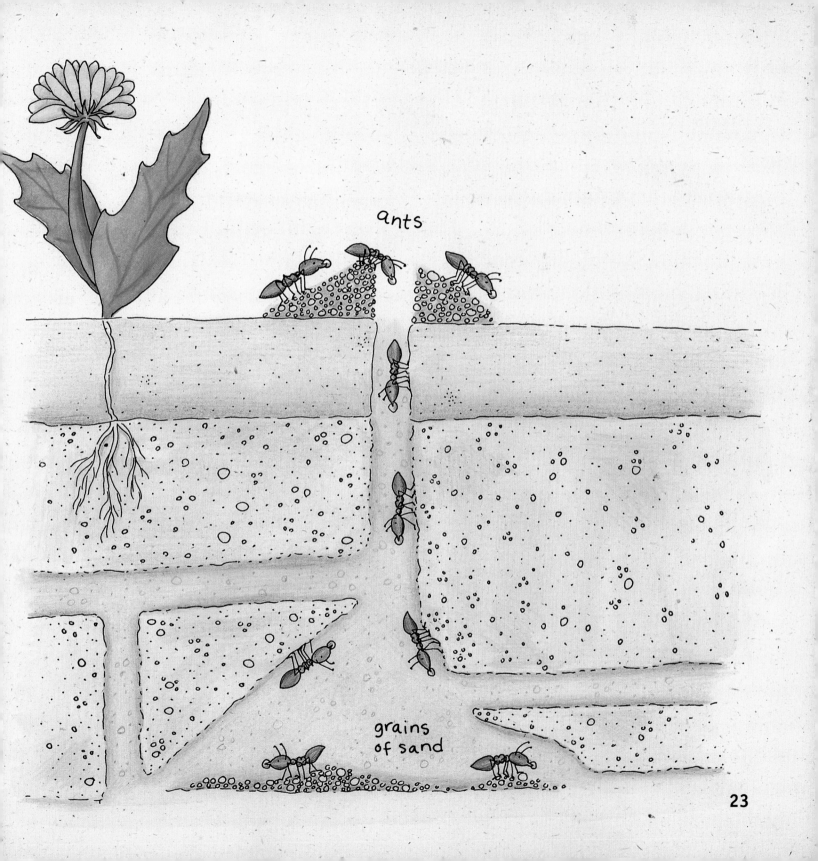

ants

grains
of sand

23

GO ON A NATURE HUNT

Be a nature detective. Go for a nature walk to your favorite place. How many of the following things can you find?

First read the entire list. Then copy the list on a pad of paper. Take the pad and pencil with you when you are ready to start your hunt. Check each item on your pad when you discover it.

1. an insect on a tree
2. an insect on a flower
3. a butterfly resting
4. a butterfly flying
5. five different kinds of wildflowers in bloom: 1 ☐ 2 ☐ 3 ☐ 4 ☐ 5 ☐
6. a tree with its treeflowers in bloom
7. green plants growing on a rock
8. green plants growing on the bark of a tree
9. clouds moving overhead
10. the branches of a tree moving in the wind
11. a bird that is flying
12. a bird building a nest
13. a bird singing
14. a bird that is hopping on the ground
15. a bird walking on the ground.
16. a closed tree bud
17. an open tree bud
18. a rock with three colors
19. a tree whose trunk is white or very light
20. a tree with a black or very dark trunk

a butterfly flying

tree branches moving in the wind

clouds moving overhead

1. an insect on a tree
2. an insect on a flower
3. a butterfly resting
4. ✓ a butterfly flying
5. five different kinds of wildflowers
   in bloom   1☐   2☐   3☐   4☐   5☐
6. a tree with its tree flowers in bloom
7. ✓ green plants growing on a rock
8. green plants growing on the bark of a tree
9. ✓ clouds moving overhead
10. the branches of a tree moving in the wind
11. a bird that is flying
12. a bird building a nest
13. a bird singing
14. a bird hopping on the ground
15. ✓ a bird walking on the ground
16. a closed tree bud
17. an open tree bud
18. a rock with three colors
19. a tree whose trunk is white or
    very light
20. a tree with a black or very dark
    trunk

a bird walking on the ground

a green plant growing on a rock

LISTEN!

You can hear all kinds of sounds outdoors if you just stop to listen. Take a pencil and pad along. You may want to make a list of all the sounds that you hear. Find a place where you can sit quietly for a while. What do you hear? Maybe a robin is singing "cheerily cheerup cheerily." Do you hear pigeons cooing? Listen for the sound made by a bird's wings as it flies past. The wings of the mourning dove create a pleasant tone when it takes off.

You may hear the peep peep peep of spring peepers. Are any ducks quacking? Can you hear bees buzzing or dogs barking? What other animal sounds do you hear?

Listen to the wind as it blows through the trees. Trees with broad leaves make a gentle clapping sound. The narrow needle leaves of a pine tree make the wind whistle as it passes through.

Sometimes trees creak and squeak when their trunks rub against each other. Perhaps you will hear the crash of a falling branch.

Can you hear water running?

Find a tree with smooth bark. Put your ear against its trunk. You may hear insects feeding inside. Perhaps you hear tree sap running.

How many sounds did you hear?

the wind whistles through pine needles

"buzzzzzzzzzzz"

"buzzzz"

"cheerily cheerup cheerily"

"peep, peep, peep"

"zzzzzz"

"zzzzzz"

"coo, coo, coo"

"peep, peep, peep"

LOOK FOR A RAINBOW

You will find a rainbow if you go outdoors at the right time and stand in the right place.

The right time is early morning or late afternoon on a rainy day. The rain has just stopped or is about ready to stop. And the sun is about ready to come out.

The right place is with the sun behind you. It is shining on your back, not on your face.

Look ahead. You should see a rainbow in front of you. It forms an arc of several colors. Red is on the outside of the arc. Orange comes next. Yellow is under the orange. The next color is green. Blue is below the green. Under the blue is indigo and then violet.

red   orange   yellow   a rainbow

green

blue

indigo

purple

INDOOR ACTIVITIES

WATCH RAINDROPS ON YOUR WINDOW

Look at the raindrops on the windowpane. Can you find which part of the raindrop is lighter and which part is darker? A raindrop acts as a lens. You see objects through it upside down. Try to look at a tree or at a pole through a raindrop. Their tops are near the ground and their bottoms appear to be up in the air.

Notice that the raindrops on the window form tiny streams. Some move faster than others. Some of the little streams join together and form bigger streams. The larger ones become heavy and plop to the bottom of the window.

Do you have a screened window? Watch the raindrops coming through the screen onto the window. Notice that they are smaller than the raindrops on the window without a screen.

raindrops on a window pane

START SPRING EARLY INDOORS

Will a spot of soil that looks bare early in spring remain bare or will plants grow there later in the season? You can find out by bringing spring indoors early. Take a flowerpot and a small shovel or trowel with you outdoors. Find a bare spot of soil. Mark the spot so that you can find it again. You can use a stake or a stone.

Dig up some of this soil and put it carefully in the flowerpot. Take the pot indoors. Spread a layer of pebbles in a dish or a tray. Place the pot on top of the pebbles.

Put all of this on or near a sunny or very bright windowsill. Do not plant anything in the soil. Just water it about once a week or when the soil feels very dry when you touch it.

Plants will probably begin to show up through the soil in a few days. Where did they come from?

Allow the plants to grow for a few weeks. Then take the pot outdoors to the spot where you dug the soil. Compare the plants in your pot with those now growing in the ground. Do any plants that are growing outdoors resemble the ones in your pot? Some may be different. How do you explain the difference?

Are the plants in your pot more developed than those growing in the ground? If they are, can you guess why that happened?

growing plants

Flower Pot

pebbles

31

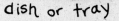
dish or tray

PLANT SEEDS UPSIDE DOWN

You can see that the leaves and stems of plants grow up, above the ground. The roots grow down in the soil.

Do you think that roots would grow up and leaves would grow down if seeds were planted upside down? You will know the answer when you try this experiment.

You will need six large seeds such as lima beans or corn grains, three jars or water glasses, two paper towels, and some water. Soak the seeds in water overnight in one of the containers.

The next day line the two empty containers with moistened paper towels. Plant three of the soaked seeds in each lined container between the glass and the wet lining, a little way from the top.

Arrange the seeds right side up in one container and upside down in the other. Pour some water into each to keep the lining moist.

The seeds will sprout in about a week. In which direction do the leaves and roots of each set of plants grow? Is there any difference between the shapes of the roots, the stems, or the leaves in each of them?

jars

lima beans

paper towels

water

lima beans soaking

lima beans' skin wrinkles after soaking

beans planted in jars with wet paper towels

 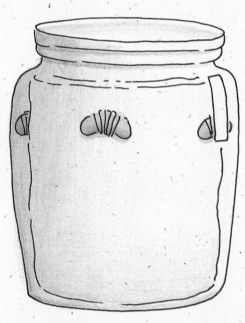

RAISE SOME PLANTS FROM A POTATO

Plants do not grow only from seeds. New plants can also grow from other parts of a plant. Try to raise some plants from a potato.

Find a potato that has several "eyes." The eyes have small buds. You can make the buds sprout in two ways.

One way is to put the potato in a black or very dark plastic bag. Place the bag in a dark closet or drawer. Look at the potato after a few weeks. How many new plants do you have?

Another way to grow sprouts from a potato is to plant it in pieces. Fill the bottom of a plant tray with moist soil. Cut several sections from a potato, each piece having one or two eyes. Plant the pieces of potato in the moist soil. Place a loose cover of aluminum foil over the top of the tray. Do not let the soil dry out.

Remove the foil after the potatoes have begun to sprout. Place them in a sunny spot. The new plants will continue to grow and turn darker green in the sunlight. You can then repot them in separate pots or plant a potato patch outdoors.

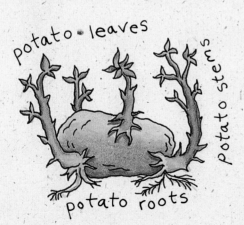

potato leaves

potato stems

potato roots

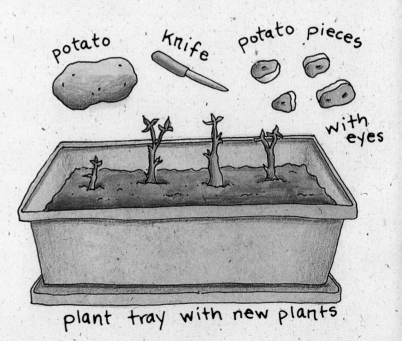

potato   knife   potato pieces

with eyes

plant tray with new plants

34

HUNT FOR SEEDS IN YOUR HOME

You may be surprised to learn how many different kinds of seeds you can find in your home. Examine the fruits and vegetables in your refrigerator. You will probably find tomatoes, cucumbers, peppers, oranges, and others that have seeds.

Do you have nuts?

Are there dried plant arrangements? Can you find the seeds in dried flowers?

Examine a bag of mixed birdseed.

How many kinds of beans do you have in your home?

Can you find any other kinds of seeds?

Collect some seeds from each source. Place each kind in a separate plastic envelope or a little bottle. How many kinds did you collect?

You may be interested in trying to grow some of these seeds. They can be planted indoors in pots or outdoors where you have a bare spot of soil. Some may produce interesting plants.

Pepper

Walnut

beans

dried flowers

tomato

GROW GRASS INDOORS

You need only four things to grow a little indoor patch of grass: a brick, a shallow tray to hold the brick, some grass seed, and water.

Wash the brick and place it in the tray. Fill the tray with water almost to the top. Place the tray in a sunny window for a few days. Check to see that there is always some water in the tray.

The water in the tray disappears quickly for two reasons. Some of it evaporates into the air. Much of it rises in the pores or tiny hoes in the brick. In a few days the entire brick will be wet.

Scatter the grass seed over the brick when it is soaked with water. You will see little shoots come up after about a week. Let the grass grow a few inches. You can trim your "lawn" with a pair of scissors.

Try to grow some food on a brick. Prepare the brick in a tray with water as explained for growing grass. Buy a package of watercress seeds in a garden shop. Scatter the seeds on the wet brick. It will take about three weeks for the cress to develop. You can harvest your crop when the plants are about three inches (eight centimeters) high. The plants are delicious in a salad or a sandwich.

wet brick with grass seeds

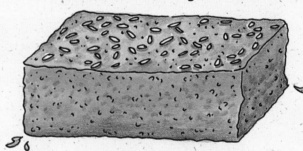

WATCH PLANTS MOVE

Plants do not move from place to place as animals do, but they do have motion. Parts of plants can twist, turn, and bend even though their roots remain firmly in the soil. Watch the movement of a geranium plant.

Put the plant in a sunny window. In a few days you will see that the leaves have moved. They turned toward the light.

The way in which clover leaves move is very interesting. Dig up a little patch of clover and put it in a saucer or a pot. Observe its leaves morning and night. The clover leaves fold over each other in a very pretty pattern as night falls.

Do flowers move? Cut a little bunch of dandelion flowers when the sun is out and the flowers are wide open. Place the stems in water. The golden flowers will remain open all day. Examine the flowers before you go to bed and after you awaken in the morning. You will find that they close as night falls. They remain closed until morning. They open once again in the daylight.

Dandelions behave in the same way outdoors. They remain closed at night and open by day. You will notice that the dandelions will also close by day if the sky becomes cloudy. They will open again if the clouds move away and the sun comes out.

You might enjoy bringing some other plants indoors to watch their movements.

cloudy   sunny

FORCE SOME PLANT BUDS TO OPEN INDOORS

Spring has arrived but it may still be cold outside. You may even find some snow on the ground. You wish that it would get warmer and that plants would begin to grow. Wouldn't you love to see some green leaves and some flowers? You can, if you start spring indoors.

First, go outside and look for trees or shrubs whose branches you can reach. Ask an adult to help you cut some twigs from several of them. The cuttings should be about the size of a new pencil.

Bring the cut twigs indoors and put each kind in a separate jar of water. Label the jars with the names of the twigs. Place the jars in a sunny window. Make a record of the date when you start this project.

Some plants that are easy to force indoors are forsythia, cherry, maple, horse chestnut, apple, dogwood. There are many others. Try to force plant buds to open on whatever twigs you can collect.

Watch the buds open. Notice the first green leaves. See the tiny leaves unfold from their neat packages. Watch how the petals open as the flowers begin to bloom.

Write the date when each type of bud opens. You will find that some buds open sooner than others. Some may not open at all. You can enjoy an early spring indoors even if you watch the opening of a single bud.

cherry

dogwood

horse chestnut

maple

39

FEED SOME EARTHWORMS

Find out what earthworms like to eat. Earthworms feed on pieces of decaying leaves and other plant parts outdoors. You can try feeding them a variety of foods when you bring some indoors.

Prepare a home for earthworms in a large deep plastic or enamel basin. Fill the container with about four inches (10 centimeters) of rich soil.

Collect some earthworms. Take a jar and a trowel or small shovel with you. Turn the soil over in a damp spot under a tree, in the woods, or in a garden to find earthworms. Put a little soil in your jar and add the earthworms. Handle them gently.

Earthworms can often be found on the top of the soil and even on paved roads if it has rained the night before. Try sprinkling some water on a patch of soil outdoors at night. Look for earthworms the next day.

Place the contents of your jar on the soil in your container at home. Place a loose cover over it. Add some food once a day for several days. Try a variety of foods such as bits of lettuce, old leaves, cornmeal, and table scraps of all kinds.

Keep a record of what you feed the worms and check off what they eat.

garden fence

jar

soil

lettuce

leaves

cornmeal

table scraps

41

HATCH SOME FROGS' EGGS

Collect some frogs' eggs and bring them home to watch them hatch.

First prepare a small aquarium with fresh water. Water from a pond is best. Tap water has chlorine and should be aired for twenty-four hours to get rid of the gas. Now you are ready to collect some eggs.

You will need a pail and a collecting net or a strainer tied to a long handle. Look for the eggs at the beginning of spring. Frogs lay their eggs in freshwater ponds. You can also find eggs in roadside puddles or in temporary pools of water.

A frogs' egg looks like a little black dot surrounded by a blob of colorless jelly. Hundreds of eggs may stick together and float in the water as one large mass. You may also find some tadpoles (also called polliwogs) in the water. These have already hatched from frogs' eggs. They look like tiny dark fishes.

Put water in your pail. Scoop up a few eggs with your net. Put them in your pail of water. Take only a few. Maybe you collected some tadpoles, too.

Take your collection home and place it in your aquarium. The eggs will probably hatch in a few days to a week. First the hind legs appear. The tadpole looks like a fish with a tail and two legs. Watch for the two front legs to grow. Now the tail begins to disappear.

Soon, in about three weeks, the tadpole will become a frog. This is a good time to take the animals back to the pond.

pail

strainer

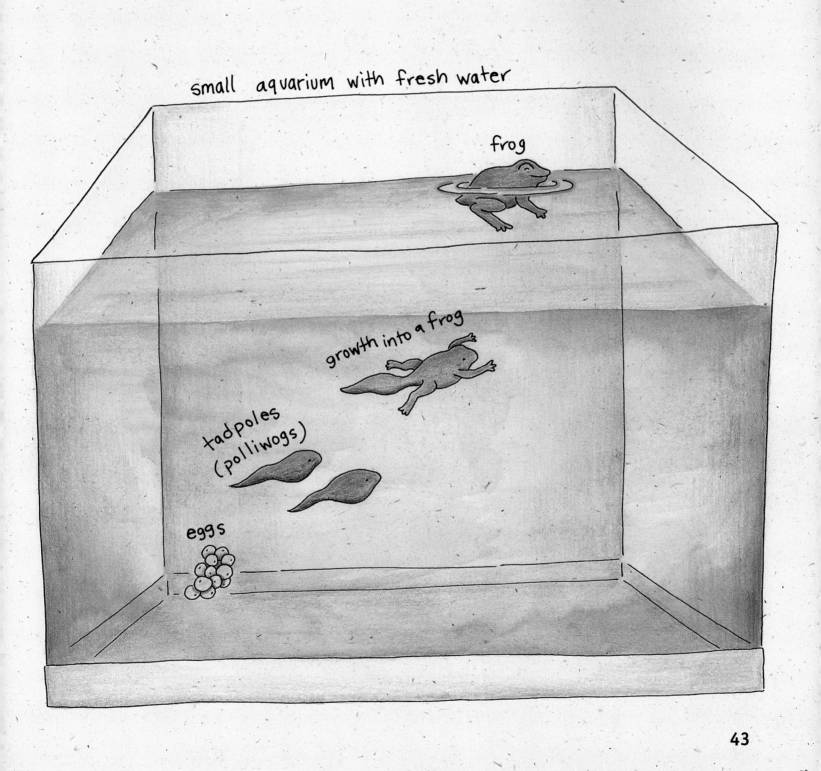

small aquarium with fresh water

frog

growth into a frog

tadpoles
(polliwogs)

eggs

43

MAKE A STONE COLLECTION

Stones found in the soil outdoors come in different colors, shapes, and textures. *Textures* means how they feel when you rub them between your fingers. Bring home twenty or more stones. Make a copy of the chart and arrange the stones as shown in the chart.

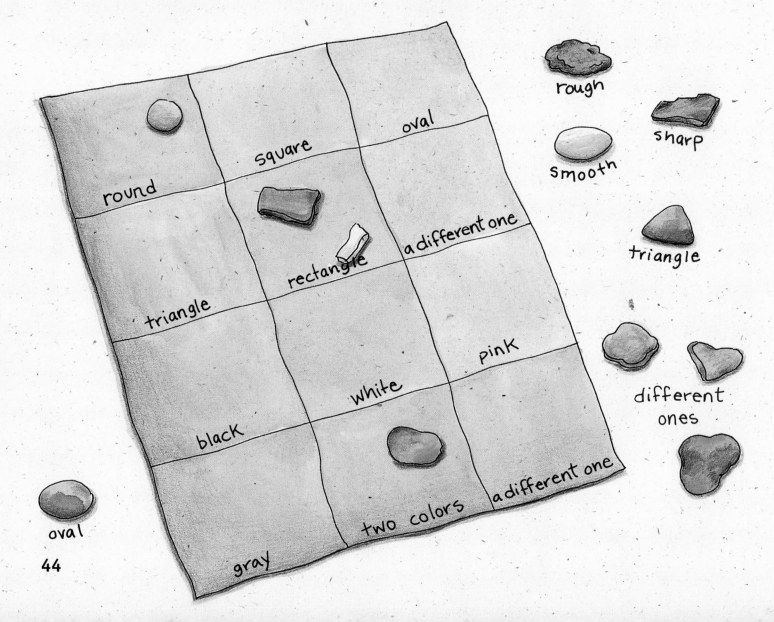

WRITE A POEM

Write a poem about your science
and nature activities. A poem may
have as few as two lines. A poem of
two lines is called a couplet.
Here are four couplets:

frog on a log

> In the pond floated a log,
> Right on top there sat a frog.
>
> I collected twenty stones.
> Some of them look like bones.
>
> Dandelions resemble gold
> When their flowers all unfold.
>
> Pour some water from a cup.
> The water falls down, never up.

dandelion

Write about what you see, hear,
smell, and feel about the world in
the spring. Look through the pages
in the book and read the index to
get some ideas. Although couplets
are fun to write, you can write
longer poems if you wish.

SOME READING SUGGESTIONS

Bailey, Jill. *How Caterpillars Turn into Butterflies.* New York: Marshall Cavendish, 1999.

Bell, Thelma Harrington. *Snow.* New York: Viking Press, 1962.

Busch, Phyllis S. *Backyard Safaris: 52 Year-Round Science Adventures.* New York: Simon and Schuster, 1995.

Chambers, Catherine. *Bark.* Chatham, N.J.: Raintree Steck-Vaughn, 1996.

Demuth, Patricia Brennan. *Cradles in the Trees: The Story of Bird Nests.* New York: Macmillan Publishing Company, 1994.

——————————. *Those Amazing Ants.* New York: Macmillan Publishing Company, 1994.

INDEX

Page numbers in boldface are illustrations